LOUIS HAYWARD

Beyond the Iron Mask

A Collective Memoir

Illustrated

By Mary Ann Anderson

BearManor
Media

Albany, Georgia

Published in the USA by
BearManor Media
P O Box 71426
Albany, Georgia 31708
www.bearmanormedia.com

Softcover Edition
ISBN: 1593939604

Printed in the United States of America

Acknowledgments

I would like to thank the following individuals for their contributions, for without them this book would not be possible:

Donna Albertsen, for the use of her rare photographs.

Paul Green, for his research on With the Marines at Tarawa.

Professor Julie Grossman, for her film reviews and encouragement.

Brian Taggert, for writing the Foreword.

Ida Lupino, for saving the letters that Louis sent to her during the war.

Shirley Phillips, for use of her article archives and research, along with removal of all the hard breaks and proofreading.

Barry Lane, for his Afterword and all his other help.

Robben Barquist, for editing.

Robbie Adkins and Allan Duffin for their typesetting.

The Marines Second Division Combat Photography Unit for their Battle of Tarawa stills.

And, special thanks to Gordon Deter, for showing me how to scan all these photo images!

foreword
By Brian Taggert

TCM's ROBERT OSBORNE CALLS IT "the va-va-voom factor." It is in the eyes, the body language, the voice and an audience responds or doesn't. Errol Flynn, Alan Ladd, Clark Gable, and James Stewart all had it on the top tier. Louis Hayward, Paul Henreid, John Hodiak, and a few others had it on the second tier.

Hayward swashbuckled his way into stardom and then made choices that were suitable for his personality. Perhaps not the best choices if one were aiming for a top star legacy, but decisions that were right for a committed actor. Correct for the man. A scoundrel in *Ladies in Retirement*, a weakling in *The Strange Woman*, a drunken lout in *Repeat Performance*. Daring choices.

And, then of course, the war when Captain Louis Hayward won the Bronze Star for heroism in capturing the Battle at Tarawa on film, one of the bloodiest beach landings of World War II.

That, of course, changed the man.

My fascination with Louis Hayward, I have autopsied over and over and finally discovered what is was, and why he resonated with me. In *The Man in The Iron Mask*, I saw the man, through movie trickery, play his twin, face to face: The foppish King Louis and his dashing brother. Two distinct personalities. How did they do that, I wondered? He did variations in *The Return of Monte Cristo*, *The Pirates of Capri*, and perhaps a few others.

This all happening when I was a young boy being raised by my grandfather, a tough studio executive at Paramount and a grandmother who was an American aristocrat. She was raising me to be a Victorian dandy, a prepubescent raconteur, and he was toughening me up in the wilds. I was fishing, hunting, a crack shot at ten, and could ride a horse like Randolph Scott. I was the living that shot in *The Man in The Iron Mask*. That is why Louis Hayward resonated with me. Which was I, the fop or the swashbuckler?

I met Louis Hayward on the set of *Chuka* with John Mills. He was charming, gracious, had the lordly laugh and the raised eyebrow. I mentioned Dirk Bogarde, whom I adored and said that I thought Bogarde was influenced by Mr. Hayward. The aristocratic laugh again, the raised eyebrow and then he said, "We were supposed to do a picture together but there was a billing problem. I'm glad I didn't do it. We would of have cancelled each other out." That laugh again, with those perfect white teeth and I realized I had come face to face with myself.

I still raise my eyebrow in emphasis and my laugh has just a hint of the haughty charm of my hero, Louis Hayward.

Table of Contents

Louis Hayward. Photo by Ernest A. Bachrach.

Chapter One
From Africa to England

CHARLES LOUIS NAPOLEON HAYWARD was born on March 19, 1909 in Johannesburg, South Africa. He was of English descent and had a large dose of French and Italian in his blood. His British born parents, Charles Hayward and Agatha Little, immigrated to South Africa.

His father, Charles was a mining engineer and prospector who took large quantities of diamonds and gold out of Transvaal. Hayward Sr. never lived to see son. Charles was accidently injured before

Transvaal Mining, South Africa, Circa 1909. Courtesy David Johnson.

Louis was born. Sadly, he was a victim of a hit and run horse drawn vehicle in 1909 and died five days after Louis was born.

In 1914, five years after her husband Charles' death and immediately before the outbreak of World War I in Europe, Louis' mother Agatha Little Hayward left South Africa. She moved back to Britain with her three children to live under the care of a wealthy uncle from Cardiff, Wales who promised to support them while they remained in London. In 1919, it was rumored that she briefly returned to South Africa and remarried. Agatha, having French roots on her mother's side, then moved with her family to France.

Louis had a brother Louis John Raynes who was a banker/cashier in Surrey, England. Louis' sister, Agatha Consuelo Hayward, who was handicapped, remained in England.

The young Hayward was brought up in the proper English manner. He went to the right preparatory schools. Louis was a star athlete engaging in football, ice hockey, golf and tennis. He also took up boxing and fencing. Louis also formed an intense and active interest in amateur dramatics. He enrolled in the Jesuit School of Sauveur in the province of Brittany, where he remained for two years. Louis concluded his college education in France. It was the general understanding that as soon as he completed his education he would go into the pit brokerage business—the manufacturing of pitch wood, used in mining operations—with his uncle in Cardiff. Louis had other ideas.

Returning to Brittany in 1927, he completed his education at the College of Redon and St. Sauveur. He graduated the following year, speaking perfect French.

Hayward persuaded his mother to finance his tuition at the Central School of Speech and Drama in London. She agreed even though there had never been an actor in the family. A fellow student was Lawrence Olivier.

"I was rummaging through some old papers and I came across a letter which the Head of the School had written to my mother.

'I feel that it is only fair to tell you that your son hasn't an iota of acting talent, 'she wrote,' and I feel that it is only fair to tell you that you are simply throwing your money away. He will never, never be an actor.'

"My mother never mentioned the letter to me. Apparently she thought that I might just as well go ahead and get the acting bug out of my system. Even when I had completed the course at the school and began to try to get a job in London, without any success whatsoever, she spoke no word of discouragement and never once urged me to give up. I used to do impressions of Charlie Chaplin for her, as a young lad at the age of six."

–*Louis Hayward*

While attending drama school, he made the rounds of theatrical agents and producers without success.

After graduation, the head master's comments appeared to be true as Hayward failed to gain interviews. Hayward spent some time managing a nightclub but he wanted to act.

"The nearest I got to a job, at this time, was the waiting bench in various producers' and agents' offices. In the afternoons, I sat around the hotels that were frequented by the old actors, listening to the romantic tales that they told. The more I heard, the more determined I was to be an actor."

–*Louis Hayward*

Chapter Two
British Theatre, British Films and Noël Coward

A DEJECTED HAYWARD STARTED HIS OWN theatrical troupe at the suggestion of an aging actor and purchased an interest in a small theatrical company. Louis' mother advanced him the money to start the troupe, which provided Hayward with the valuable experience of acting on the stage with a small degree of recognition. He appeared in Camille, Moths, and East Lynne.

Actor and producer Gerald Du Maurier saw him in one of these productions and he was impressed with the stage presence,

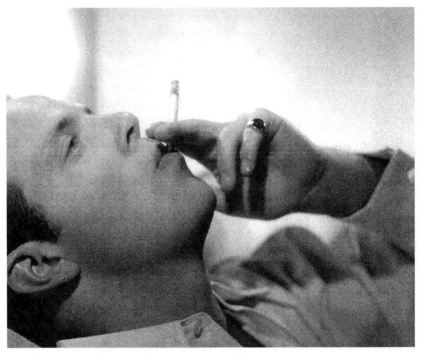

fluidity of movement, and dash displayed by Louis. Du Maurier offered him a part in *The Church Mouse*, which was produced in the West End of London in 1929.

After the close of *The Church Mouse*, Louis again went on tour, this time playing the youngest brother in a production of *Beau Geste*. He stayed with this play for a year. Hayward was convinced that his future was in London so he sold his interest in his touring company.

This led to a role in the 1931 West End production of *Dracula*. Louis portrayed Renfield on the stage of the Prince of Wales Theatre.

When *Dracula* closed, an exhausted Louis had saved enough money to take a holiday. Hayward journeyed to Corsica and for the next year led a nomadic life on the island.

When Hayward returned to London in 1932, the young, five-foot-eleven-inch, blue-eyed and dark-haired actor finally found success.

One night, while Hayward was appearing in a play with Gerald Du Maurier, Noël Coward happened to be in the audience. Noël liked Hayward's work and sent him a note back stage.

"If you ever need a job," he wrote, "come and see me."

Meeting with the noted British playwright, Noël Coward was the catalyst of a life-changing friendship. Coward cast Hayward as the male lead in his new play *Conversation Piece*, which starred the French actress Yvonne Printemps. This production was a success on the London stage.

Hayward then made his film debut in support of Heather Angel in *Self Made Lady* (1932, United Artist - British). Directed by George King, the film stars Heather Angel, Henry Wilcoxon, Amy Veness, A. Bromley Davenport, Charles Cullum, Ronald Ritchie, Doris Gilmore, Lola Duncan, Oriel Ross, and Violet Hopson. Louis portrays the part of a wealthy young man, Paul Geneste, who vies without success against Henry Wilcoxon for the hand of Angel.

Other films followed: *The Man Outside* (1933, RKO-British) was directed by George A. Cooper. It stars Henry Kendall, Gillian Lind, Joan Gardner, Michael Hogan, Cyril Raymond, John Turnbull and Ethel Warrick. Louis Hayward portrays the character of Frank Elford.

I'll Stick to You (1933, British Lion) was directed by Leslie Hiscott. The film stars Jay Laurier, Betty Astell, Ernest Sefton, Hal

Walters, Annie Esmond, Mary Gaskell and Charles Childerstone. Louis Hayward plays Ronnie Mathews.

The Thirteenth Candle (1933, Warner Bros. British) was directed by John Daumery and stars Isobel Elsom, Arthur Maude, Gibb McLaughlin, Joyce Kirby, Louis Goodrich, D. A. Clarke-Smith, Winifred Oughton, Claude Fleming, Charles Childerstone, and Hilliard Vox. Louis Hayward portrays Paul Marriott, a murder suspect.

Chelsea Life (1933, Paramount – British) was directed by Sidney Morgan. It features actors Molly Johnson, Anna Lee, Kathleen Saxon, Stanley Vilven, Gordon McLeod, Eric Hales, Patrick Ludlow, Arthur Chesney, and Quentin McPhearson. Louis Hayward portrays David Fenner, a struggling artist.

Sorrell and Son (1933, United Artists – British), directed by Jack Raymond, stars H.B. Warner, Hugh Williams, Winifred Shotter, Margot Grahame, Donald Calthrop, Ruby Miller, Evelyn Roberts, Arthur Chesney, Wally Patch and Hope Davy. Louis Hayward portrays Duncan, a student.

The Love Test (1935, Fox – British), by director Michael Powell, features Judy Gunn, David Hutcheson, Morris Harvey, Googie Withers, Aubrey Dexter, Eve Turner, Jack Knight, Shayle Gardner, and Bernard Miles. Louis Hayward portrays John Gregg, a young inventor.

Noël Coward cast Louis again in his revival of his 1925 hit *Hay Fever*, which starred Constance Collier.

Noël boosted Hayward's career once again by writing *Point Valaine*, a three act play with seven scenes, which had premiered in

Point Valaine (1935) Osgood Perkins, Louis Hayward, Lynn Fontaine
and Alfred Lunt

Boston in 1934 and opened January 16, 1935 and ran only fifty-five
performances. It was reproduced later in Britain in 1947.

A line from the play, written by Noël Coward, "Kick away all
you like. Snap out of your deep romantic despair and be a man,
my son!"Louis was working with Alfred Lund and Lynn Fontaine.
Hayward's performance in this production at the Ethel Barrymore
Theater won him the Vanity Fair Award for Best Stage Performance of the Year.

Hayward was allegedly having a homosexual affair with Coward, an affair that came between Louis and an American girl, who

was visiting in London. He had fallen head over heels in love with this girl. It was rumored that Louis chose Noël.

"Noël Coward offered to write a role for me in a play he was doing with Alfred Lunt and Lynn Fontaine. It was an offer I could not refuse. By the time I finally got to New York, well you know how these things are—absence makes the heart grow fonder in spite of what the poets say—at any rate, things were different when I saw the girl again."

–Louis Hayward

This play was certainly a new departure for Noël Coward, recalling W. Somerset Maugham with its heady tropical atmosphere and the thwarted passions of a female hotel owner, her Slav lover and various other guests. As if to stress the difference between this and earlier, more innocuous offerings, Coward sprinkled his play with bad language—"bastard" and "bloody." This was an American production and not subject to Cromer's (the play's previous producer) blue pencil.

"I was honestly attempting to break new ground by creating a group of characters establishing atmosphere as far removed as possible from anything I have done before."

–Noël Coward

MGM - One Big Happy Family

There is also a sexually ambiguous male couple and a visiting writer, Mortimer Quinn, perhaps an evocation of the play's spiritual father, W. Somerset Maugham, a man whom Coward would see as increasingly bitter even as he plundered the world for material.

"I always affect to despise human nature. My role in life is so clearly marked; cynical, detached, unscrupulous, an ironic observer and recorder of other's people's passions. It is a nice façade to sit behind but trifle bleak. What discourages me the most is confusion. The dreary capacity of the human race for putting the right labels on the wrong boxes."

– Noël Coward

Coward admits the play was written out of an "innocent desire to create two whopping and good parts for the Lunts," which it did, but Coward failed to write a good enough story to show off these parts—a dilemma Noël had faced in his "affair" with Louis Hayward.

His relationship with Louis Hayward ended bitterly. Hayward's ability to make Coward jealous was well demonstrated when he had a ship board romance with Natasha Paley, Jack Wilson's wife to be.

According to Noël Coward, adapted from his diaries by Phillip Hoare:

"Chartering a yacht, the Mara, and a crew, Coward set sail for Cannes. Aboard was his new friend, a handsome young actor named Louis Hayward. They had met two years previously when Hayward was appearing in Another Language, at the Lyric Theatre. Hayward was ten years younger than Coward, whom Coward called, "Sugar." Noel found Louis irresistible; a sequence of photograph's in Noël's album show Hayward riding horseback and leaping fences, romantic in shirtsleeves and breaches."

"What ought to have been a romantic sail along the Italian coast ended up in disaster. They anchored off of Corsica at L'ile Rousse, where a violent storm blew up while they were ashore, breaking the yacht against the rocks. Noel and his crew had to walk twenty miles to find help. Coward dramatizes the scene with the failing French Captain and himself taking the boat's wheel, 'up held gin and my ex-appendicitis truss.' In fact, Hayward and he merely waded out to the wreck, the following day to retrieve what they could. Noël had lost his typewriter, passport, money, clothes and more importantly the manuscript of his biography."

Many years later, when Hayward was making a television series of *The Saint,* on stage next door was Coward; the bitterness had evidently endured: Noël wouldn't even talk to Hayward. Louis was married to actress Ida Lupino at the time.

> "It was emphatically not one of the happier episodes of my life!"
>
> *–Noël Coward*

> "I use to channel Noël and imitate him when I played gay parts."
>
> *–Louis Hayward*

Chapter Three
Hollywood

HOLLYWOOD WAS THE NEXT STEP, for Louis was young, attractive and had plenty of charm. Hayward starred in *Self Made Lady* for United Artists. Then came the young dipsomaniacal role in *The Flame Within,* co-staring Ann Harding and Herbert Marshall. Louis played the alcoholic Jack Kerry, who is eventually reformed by Ann Harding as Doctor Mary White. Hayward gained excellent notices for this role.

Saturday, November 23, 1935 Seattle Daily Times (Seattle, Washington)

FILM OF LONDON

NOW AT LIBERTY

A Feather in Her Hat is currently showing at The Liberty Theatre.

In the film, Pauline Lord, Basil Rathbone, Louis Hayward, Billie Burke, Wendy Barrie, Victor Varconi and others acted as if they were not on the screen at all, but in the heart of London, where the action takes place.

Miss Lord's performance of Clarissa Phelps leaves nothing to be desired. It is always apparent that she is enjoying the role as much as the audience. Rathbone, as the rum-soaked but genteel Captain Courtney, to whom she gives shelter so he may rear her lower-class son to be a gentleman, conducts himself as an experienced actor might. Louis Hayward, the son, becomes a decided threat to Hollywood's currently favored juveniles.

Billie Burke, playing the actress to whom Clarissa sacrifices her son so that he may live with the upper class, does her best performance to date, continually distressed and fluttery. Miss Burke, with whom the son falls in love, makes every man in the audience envy Hayward. And, Varconi, Teutonic and bewildered, plays his part in turn.

Directed by Alfred Santell and adapted by Lawrence Hazard, *A Feather in Her Hat* emerges as an extraordinary play on emotion.

Hayward was loaned out to Columbia for *A Feather In Her Hat*. He and Wendy Barrie, also in the cast, became romantically involved but despite the experiences of some, the couple did not marry—reportedly due to his "fling" with Noël Coward.

Ironically enough, he played this role so effectively that, thereafter, nobody could seem to visualize him in any other kind of role. The result was he spent most of his time sitting around waiting for someone to tailor another good dipsomaniac role. Louis was cast in *Trouble For Two* (1936, Metro Goldwyn Meyer) as a murder victim. The film was directed by J. Walter Ruben and starred Robert Montgomery, Rosalind Russell, Frank Morgan, and Reginald Owen.

Back at MGM, Louis Hayward appeared in *Absolute Quiet*, which was directed by George B. Seitz. The screenplay was adapted by Harry Clork from the story by George F. Worts. Hayward starred alongside Raymond Walburn, Lionel Atwill, Stuart Erwin, Irene Hervey, and Ann Loring.

Louis concluded his contract with another loan out, this time to Warner Bros., for the part of the young father in *Anthony Adverse*.

Tuesday, August 25, 1936 *Dallas Morning News* Dallas Texas:

"ANTHONY ADVERSE"

Actually Becomes A Movie Production

Filmdom Takes Over This Thing by Harvey Allen:

Only Half Million Feet Necessary

By Sheilah Graham

Special Correspondent of News

A Feather in Her Hat (1935) Louis Hayward and Basil Rathbone

HOLLYWOOD, Calif. Aug. 24, - "Anthony Adverse"..... In production in ninety days... 500,000 feet of film were used, reduced to 14,000 feet.... Length of performance, two hours and twenty minutes....Claude Rains (Don Louis) and Louis Hayward (Denis) were allow one week only to learn how to fence. As a result Rains cut Hayward's forehead open and pierced his trousers above the knee, drawing blood.

Louis has his defining moment and makes an impact with the audiences in his portrayal of the dashing Officer Denis Moore, Anthony's father in this romantic prologue Anthony Adverse. Scenes were shot with gauze to create the dream-like romantic interlude of the lovers. He rescues his soon-to-be mother, Maria, from an arranged marriage to Marquis Don Luis, who is brilliantly portrayed by Claude Rains. This film's prologue played to the bitter end with Hayward dispatched by luck in a sword duel with the outraged Don Luis and Maria, now pregnant and forced to return to her husband.

Louis then signed a contract with Universal and the studio cast him in a gay little comedy called *The Luckiest Girl in the World* (1936, Universal). Directed by Eddie Buzzell and starring Jane Wyatt, the film finally broke the dipsomaniac jinx for Louis Hayward. He played the gambler Anthony McClellan. Hayward would again play a similar role as Barry Gilbert in *Midnight Intruder* (1936, Universal).

The Stars of *A Feather in Her Hat*

RKO RADIO's Spectacular *The Woman I Love*

(1936)

Hayward heads the cast of Hollywood favorites in
a setting of Paris and a French flying field up the lines
during a major attack. He is in a love feud of the air with
Paul Muni, a member of the flying team on the French
front during World War. They are rivals for the same
woman, the role portrayed by Miriam Hopkins, the wife
of one of the flying team members. Anatole Litvak director of the French film based on the same story by Joseph
Kessel was brought to this country by RKO in the same
capacity.

In 1938, Jack Dunn, an ice hockey star and personal friend of Louis was set to make his motion picture debut for producer Edward Small in *The Duke of West Point*, which was directed by Alfred E. Green and starred Joan Fontaine.

Tragically, Dunn fell ill and died before the production got under way. Louis, athletic and able to skate, an ability which was required for the part in this film, was hired as a replacement. Green wanted Hayward to give Fontaine a "playboy kiss." Green admitted he could not describe the kiss in words but he knew the difference, so Louis challenged the director to give a demonstration of kisses with Miss Fontaine as the judge. It seems that Green's idea of a playboy was being just a little fresh and slightly more animated than usual, but unfortunately, it was not to Miss Fontaine's liking:

> "I guess I'm not the playgirl type. There is a kind of kissing that is natural and beautiful. The playboy kiss does not fall into this category."

Being a good trouper, Miss Fontaine elected to follow the director's orders, so Hayward, much to his embarrassment, went through eleven rehearsals and takes before he satisfied Director Green with his playboy kiss.

Hundreds of Hollywood extras were hired for the large crowd scene to depict the life of the cadets at West Point accurately and authentically.

Anthony Adverse Warner Bros. (1936). Anita Louise and Louis Hayward.

Saturday, March 11, 1939 Register-Republic
(Rockford, Illinois)
SHOW AN ACTOR FIGHTING DUEL WITH HIMSELF

HOLLYWOOD – (INS) – All of Hollywood's magic will go into the making of Edward Small's production of "The Man in the Iron Mask," highlighted when Louis Hayward, as King Louis XIV of France, fights a duel with himself as Philippe, his twin brother.*

This will be accomplished by a mask of Hayward made by Perc Westmore, one of the screen's most famous make-up experts. Except for its sinister experience - for King Louis is the bad brother and Philippe the good brother - you can't tell him from Hayward's own face. Westmore, head of Warner's make-up department, regards the recreation of Hayward's face in a life-like rubber composition as one of the accomplishments in movie make-believe.

Brief Synopsis: The Man in the Iron Mask
"Alexandre Dumas most amazing, adventurous epic."

The Man in the Iron Mask has a long cinematic history. There have been many screen adaptations of this classic 19th century novel by Alexander Dumas, dating all the way back to 1909.

Louis Hayward, a romantic lead, has just learned that Miriam Hopkins is the wife of a flying companion, Paul Muni, in this sequence of RKO Radio's *The Woman I Love* (1937). Director Anatole Litvak looks on approvingly, as she explains she "respected but never loved" the older man. Cameraman Eddie Pyle (background) watches the rehearsal.

The movie begins with the birth of twin sons to King Louis XIII in 17th Century France.

One son is the dauphin and the other son is secretly sent away to be raised in Gascony by the Kings friend and confident d' Astagnan.

The film then jumps ahead twenty years where fate brings the twins together:

The twin brother of King Louis XIV, Phillippe of Gascony, is illegally imprisoned because his very existence, real and imagined, seems to justifiably threaten the king's corrupt reign. Raised by D'Artagan and The Musketeers, Phillippe, is played by Louis Hayward in a reflection of his own personality.

As Philip of Gascony, he is gentle and unassuming with a very different demeanor with a different voice.

The other brother, Louis XIV, also played by Louis Hayward, burlesques Noel Coward's most fey vocal and physical mannerisms, creating what must be considered the definitive performance of its kind.

The arrogant King, he is foppish, cruel, dismissive and lustful.

The story itself has been modified from the original Dumas recognizing the impending war in Europe with a bit of wild west and Prisoner of Zenda-like story telling thrown in. All this is complemented by Lucien Moraweck's Academy Award nominated score, James Whale's visual ideas, and a grand cast headed by Warren William as D'Artaganan, Joseph Schildkraut as the conniving finance minister, Fouquet.

Joan Bennett, portrays Princess Maria Theresa - the quintessential damsel in distress, to be fought for, loved and admired in perpetuity.

Alan Curtis as Cadet Strong is displeased to discover Louis Hayward, as Steve Early, courting Curtis' date, Joan Fontaine, as Ann Porter, after the lights had suddenly and mysteriously been switched off during a dance – a scene from the film *The Duke of West Point*.

Alan Hale made a career of playing Porthos or Porthos-like characters often called Little john or Leperello. His son, Alan Hale, Jr. carried on the family tradition playing the Porthos in *At Sword's Point*, *The Fifth Musketeer* and *Lady In the Iron Mask*, produced by Joan Bennett's husband Walter Wanger while serving time in prison for shooting Jennings Lang, his wife's agent. But, that is another story, and a pretty good one.

The Duke of West Point

George MacDonald Fraser, author of *The Flashman* series, as well as screenwriter of *Octopussy*. Three Musketeer masterpieces directed by Richard Lester wanted Louis to play D 'Artaganan's father in the first of these. Joss Ackland played that part but in

Hayward made a tremendous impact with audiences when he starred in _The Man in the Iron Mask_ (1939, United Artists), portraying the dual role of twin brothers—one good and one evil.

The Man in the Iron Mask

the course of our conversations. Mr. Fraser introduced me to Jeffrey Richards and his omnibus volume, *Swordsmen Of The Screen* in which he observed that "producer Edward Small has seemingly cornered the market in Dumas adaptations."

In George Bruce's adaptation for Small, Fouquet, who in the Dumas original had been treated sympathetically became the villian. Colbert, who had been up to no good, became an almost avuncular screen presence.

The Iron Mask itself was made of copper, which gave Louis Hayward a skin infection shutting down production for several days.

Louis Hayward in what would be his biggest and challenging role - does a brilliant job with impressive flair playing both royal twins, the pampered and murderous king and his brave, empathetic hounded brother - a finer man than he will ever be.

Variety called *The Man in the Iron Mask* "a highly entertaining adventure with "excelent" direction."

Louis was perfectly at ease in period costume. He engaged in heroics and sword play while romancing the beauteous Joan Bennett, who portrays Maria Theresa, the Spanish infant who becomes King Louis' queen, with dash and a mocking smile. Theresa hates her husband in this marriage of state but falls desperately in love with Philippe.

Hayward will walk around himself so that it will be obvious to the audience that both men are the same person. Trick photography will accomplish new miracles on the screen in scenes with Louis playing both parts. The dueling scene will be the only one in which Hayward does not appear on the screen as both brothers. Albert Cravens, expert swordsman and a man of Hayward's exact physique will wear the mask in the duel. Hayward and other cast members are being instructed in swordsmanship by Craven's father, Fred who has taught Ramon Novarro, Tyrone Powers and many other stars

The voices will overlap. Hayward will talk in a higher pitch as the King.

Small's production is similar to the 1921 production of *The Three Musketeers* featuring Douglas Fairbanks, Sr., in which he played D'Artagnan, the principle character in that version. Warren William played the new D'Artagnan. Louis was destined to become a new Douglas Fairbanks.

Excerpt from *Peter Cushing: An Autobiography* and *Past Forgetting*:

"I got to know Louis Hayward very well when we were working together on *The Man with The Iron Mask* and we were firm friends. He struck me as a somewhat sad and lonely soul, disenchanted with the film business, who seemed glad to have someone to talk about 'the Old Country'. He was married to Ida Lupino and living in a delightful villa on the Brentwood Heights, about half way between the film capital and Santa Monica. I spent many enjoyable weekends there and finally they kindly invited me to stay with them for as long as I wished."

—*Peter Cushing*

Hayward's next film was *My Son My Son!* Critics lavished his performance but the public was confused at the sudden change in character for the newly found romantic star. Film historians feel this was not the right move for an actor so early in his career, who needed to establish a screen identity first.

Hayward was then loaned out to RKO for *Dance, Girl, Dance,* which was directed by Dorothy Arzner and featured music by Edward Ward. Louis appeared alongside Maureen O'Hara, as the ballerina Judy O'Brien, and Lucille Ball, as Bubbles, a burlesque queen.

Professor Julie Grossman, of the Department of English, Communications, and Film Studies at Le Moyne College elaborates on the significance of the film:

> In "Dance, Girl, Dance" (Dorothy Arzner, 1940) Louis Hayward plays the earnest but rich Jimmy Harris, who is on the rebound from Elinor (Virginia Field), the wife he still loves. Jimmy is drawn, even within his despair, to Judy O'Brien (Maureen O'Hara), whose innocence speaks to his own vulnerability. Amidst a sexually exploitative world of show dancing and ogling at women's bodies, Jimmy Harris twice stands up for Judy and her colleagues. The first time they meet is at a dance club just busted on gambling charges. Judy exhorts the police officer to allow the women to insist they be paid, and Jimmy lobbies for donations from the crowd to pay the women some approximation of their deserved wages. Jimmy calls the dancers "innocent victims of a man's avarice" and charms Judy through

his generous appeal on the women's behalf. "How would you like to dance your feet off for a jaded public and not get paid!" Judy falls for Jimmy Harris even before he compares her to the morning star, "the one that keeps shining after all the others have quit."

Later in the film, Judy is traumatized by her failure to become a dance artist (and the realization that Jimmy is still in love with Elinor). Judy's colleague "Bubbles" (Lucille Ball), however, makes it big by playing "Tiger Lily White" in a burlesque extravaganza. In the show, Judy is hired to whip up excitement for Lily's routine by dancing a high-toned ballet to a lascivious crowd of hecklers before Bubbles comes on the stage. Once again, Jimmy Harris appears to censure the crowd. "Give the little lady a break," he yells; "what's the matter with you guys; you're mixing her up!" Jimmy not only lessons the audience for heckling, he goes right to the stage and encourages Judy O'Brien directly. "Don't let em get you down. You keep right on," he encourages her. "That's the ticket. Show em' you can take it."

His implied critique of voyeurism serves as a unique complement to Judy's subsequent speech to the audience – a shocking lambasting of show-goers for spending "fifty cents" (to stare) at a girl the way your wives won't let you. Jimmy's appreciation for the film's heroine and Louis Hayward's charm are all the more winning and interesting because Jimmy and Judy don't end up together.

My Son, My Son! Maeve (Laraine Day) burlesques a scene she did as a child, for the benefit of her brother, Rory (Bruce Lester) and Oliver Essex (Louis Hayward). A scene from *My Son, My Son!* An Edward Small production for United Artists release, directed by Charles Vidor. The cast includes Madeleine Carroll, Brian Aherne, Henry Hull and Josephine Hutchinson.

Scene from *Dance Girl Dance*

Scene from *Dance Girl Dance*

Louis Hayward and Lucille Ball

Louis Hayward and Lucille Ball

At the end of this cinematic gem, Jimmy reunites with his wife, and Judy earns a shot at being a real artist and ballet dancer.

—*Professor Julie Grossman,*
Film Studies Le Moyne College

After the release of *The Son of Monte Cristo,* a sword was in Hayward's hand from then on. Louis Hayward was rated one of Hollywood's top ten box office stars. He was then cast in *The Return of Monte Cristo* (which was alternatively known as *Monte Cristo's Revenge*). Louis settled into these starring parts and adventure stories.

Louis Hayward is swashbuckling up at the Byrd this week in another chapter from the chronicles of the fabulous Monte Cristo family. This story is called, "The Return of Monte Cristo" but aside from the title and time element, it's the game adventure flamboyant, delightful implausible yarn it always has been.

The original Edmond Dantes, if you remember, was a fellow who escaped from the dread Château D'If, discovered a fortune and returned to France to kill off his former persecutors, one by one, dispensing largesse as he went along. Now another Edmund, a grand-nephew, turns up to claim his fortune, is unceremoniously hustled off to Devil's Island on trumped up charges, escapes and comes home to kill off his own trio of scoundrels. Barbara Britton looks exceedingly pretty as Hayward's romantic interest.

In 1941, Louis Hayward made his last Hollywood film until after the war, before enlisting in the Marines (a move that would profoundly affect his life and career): *Ladies in Retirement (*1941,

Columbia Pictures), directed by Charles Vidor. He co-starred with his wife at the time, acclaimed actress Ida Lupino (Ellen Creed), Elsa Lanchester (Emily), Evelyn Keyes (Lucy), Isobel Elsom (Leonora Fiske) and Edith Barrett (Louisa).

"Ladies In Retirement" is an intriguing role for Hayward because as in Dance, Girl, Dance the year before, directed by Dorothy Arzner, he is the male outlier in a story where women take center stage, not overly common in classic Hollywood film.

–Professor Julie Grossman

This presentation of this spine chiller closely follows the action of the Broadway and London play written by Edward Percy and Reginald Denham, that opened in New York on March 26, 1940 and closed August 3rd rather than going on for a couple of months.

'Men's as scarce here as hansom cabs. We're a covey of old women. There's only the nuns down at the priory and us.'

Gilbert Miller, who produced of the play, was the picture's co-producer. Here on the marshes of London is the story of Ellen, portrayed by Ida Lupino, who in order to keep her two older feeble minded sisters from being sent to an asylum craftily kills her employer, an ex-actress, hoping to provide a permanent home for them.

REAL DISGUISE – Portraying six separate persons comes easy to talented Louis Hayward, male star of Columbia's *The Return of Monte Cristo*. Here, he is seen as Louis Napoleon, Emperor of France, one of the disguises he is called upon to assume in the story.

LETTER PERFECT – Louis Hayward (left) and Steven Geray study their lines Columbia's *The Return of Monte Cristo*, based on characters created by the immortal Alexandre Dumas.

ROMANTIC LEADS – Dashing Louis Hayward and lovely Barbara Britton are the co-stars of Columbia's dramatic adventure story, *The Return of Monte Cristo*, based on characters created by Alexandre Dumas.

Her deed is discovered by her rascal nephew, portrayed by Louis Hayward.

In the film, after detecting the strange tones of a 'man's voice – it's so funny, here.' Lucy runs into the living room to meet Albert Feather. The motif of female space and male incursion is humorously reinforced when Albert appears later in the film and Ellen's sister shrieks as if in fear when he comes into the house from the rain.

Indeed, when Hayward first appears in the film, he is cleverly framed by director Charles Vidor, through the window of the house, watching Miss Fiske from outside. On the lam from a Gravesend bank where he stole 100 pounds, Albert is the unlikely nephew by marriage to steely Aunt Ellen, played by Ida Lupino. Milking 12 pounds from Miss Fiske, Albert jauntily sings from The Mikado, "Oh, willow, titwillow, titwillow!" and the British music hall favorite, "It's the Same the World Over" seducing Lucy with, "You don't have to know people to kiss them!" Later, he enlists her to aid him in his plan to abscond from the house after stealing the women's money. The film's strange energy derives in large part from the contrast between Lupino's and Hayward's performances. As always, Lupino is charismatic but her icy demeanor as Ellen is belied by her fierce passion for keeping her eccentric sisters Emily and Louisa safe from unsympathetic authority figures. First: Ellen brings them to the Fiske household to avoid being sent to an asylum by

A scene from *Ladies in Retirement*.

Albert Feather and Auntie Ellen

uncaring landlords in London. Second: Ellen then mur-
ders the smug and wealthy Miss Fiske when the latter
demands that Ellen's sisters be sent away. Hayward's character, Albert Feather, is, as his name suggests, a superficial
but charming cad seeking easy money and a safe haven.
Louisa comments after playing cribbage with him that
"of course Albert cheated but it was rather fun watching him cheat." It is this weird blend of tones in "Ladies
In Retirement" that intrigues. Hayward's exuberance and
insinuating sexual presence complements Lupino's grav-
ity. 'Think of all the fun Ellen is missing,' says Albert. He
repeatedly goads Ellen, Vidor often framing him in close
shots in which he sidles up to Ellen and Lucy. Throughout the film Albert archly calls her "my loving auntie" and
himself her "long- lost nephew."

And Then There Were None

In 1941, Lupino was 23, and Hayward was 32.

–Professor Julie Grossman,

Film Studies Le Moyne College

Hayward's next film, *And Then There Were None* (1945, 20th Century-Fox), was produced by Harry M. Popkin and directed by Rene Clair. Screenwriter Dudley Nichols adapted the script from the bestselling novel written by Agatha Christie. As the film opens, a boat silently makes its way toward a dark mansion on a rocky island. In the boat are eight strangely assorted passengers, Lombard portrayed by Louis Hayward, June Duprez as Vera Claythorne, Dr. Armstrong (Walter Huston), Judge Quincannon (Barry Fitzgerald), General Mandrake (Sir Aubrey Smith), Detective William Bloor (Roland Young), Emily Brent (Judith Anderson), and Prince Starloff (Mischa Auer).

Sunday, March 6, 1938 Springfield Republican

(Springfield, Massachusetts)

LOUIS HAYWARD CAST

IN 'THE SAINT IN NEW YORK'

Louis Hayward, personable young British born actor, has been awarded the top role in RKO's forthcoming feature, "The Saint in New York," which William Sistrom will produce with Ben Holmes handling the megaphone. Eduardo CiancIli also will have an important part.

Based on one of the series of popular mystery stories by Leslie Charteris, "The Saint in New York" centers around the one-man activities of Simon Templar (The Saint) to rid New York of its underworld leaders. Anthon Veiller and Charles Kaufman wrote the script.

The Saint Films

Louis Hayward also gained attention for his role as Simon Templar in Leslie Charteris' *The Saint in New York* (1938). His portrayal gave viewers a darker, more sinister Templar than in later versions that have become cult classics. Hayward portrayed The Saint again in 1940.

In 1953, Louis journeyed off to England to reprise his role as the Saint in *The Saint's Return*, shown in the United States as *The Saint's Girl Friday*. Sadly, it did not generate further interest in a film series, although later it did very well when brought to television with Roger Moore starring.

Brian Aherne, Hayward's co-star in *My Son, My Son!*, would also play The Saint in 1945 for RKO's radio broadcast adaptation.

The Saint in New York 1938
RKO Radio Pictures- USA 69 minutes – 6273 feet
Released in the USA on June 3, 1938

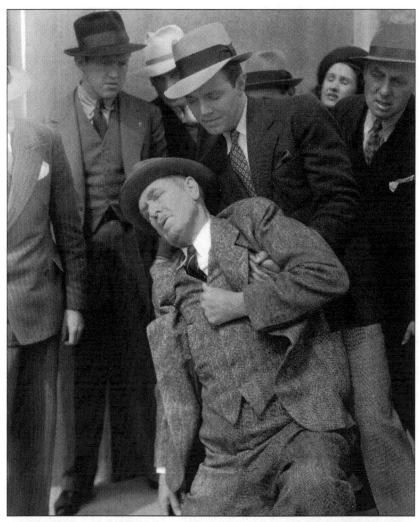

Louis Hayward and Fred Burton are shown in a scene from RKO Radio's *The Saint In New York* **in which Hayward heads the cast with Kay Sutton as the feminine lead.**

Romantically teamed in an exciting screen adventure, Louis Hayward and Naomi Chance.

Adapted from Leslie Charteris' novel *The Saint in New York* (15-B27, 1935)

Directed by Ben Holme

Produced by William Sistrom

Screenplay by Charles Kaufman and Mortimer Offner.

Starring Louis Hayward as Simon Templer, Kay Sutton as Fay Edwards, Sig Rumann as Hutch Rellin,

Jonathan Hale as inspector Fernack and Jack Carson as Red Jenks.

The Saint's Return 1953

The Saint's Girl Friday 1954

Distributed in the United Kingdom by Royal Productions

Exclusive films as The Saint' Return

73 minutes 6583 feet

Released in the UK on October 12, 1953.

Distributed by RKO Pictures in the USA as *The Saint's Girl Friday*

68 minutes 6132 feet

Released in the USA on April 15, 1954

Directed by Seymour Friedman

Produced by Julian Lesser and Anthony Hinds

Screenplay by Allan MacKennon

Starring Louis Hayward as Simon Templar, Naomi Chance as Carol Denby, Sidney Taffler as Max Lennar,

Diane Dors as Marge Russell Enoch as Keith Merton and Charles Victor as Chief inspector Teal.

RKO wished to purchase his contract from Universal and star him in a series of Saint Films. Louis demanded more money than RKO would pay and George Sanders became a new Saint. Hayward concluded his Universal pact with the role of the charming though playboy in *The Rage of Paris*, an excellently received comedy.

Chapter Four
Ida and Louis: The Inner War

WITH HIS CAREER ON THE RISE, Louis married Ida Lupino in 1938, with whom he co-starred in the memorable Ladies in Retirement. This was one of Ida's all-time favorite movies. Hayward first met Ida on a movie set at Elstree Studios in England four years earlier. Ida was not impressed at their first meeting.

> "I thought he was the dullest person I'd ever met. He seemed to run with the theatre crowd. He bored me to extinction. The feeling was utterly mutual."

A few years later they met again in Hollywood. Hayward was renting an apartment in the Hollywood Hills with his friend, Felix Tossort. This apartment was located near Ida's home on Chislehurst Drive. After Felix formed a friendship with Ida's cousin Barry Lupino, he was invited to her home. Ida had no idea Felix was sharing an apartment with Louis Hayward but eventually reconnected with him. This time around, their mutual boredom turned into mutual attraction.

"Something snapped in both of us," described Ida.

Louis and Ida experienced many conflicts in their marriage, according to Lupino, and they kept separate bedrooms.

"I had become the bigger star and with Louis' help and encouragement! We almost never see a picture," Ida confessed. "You'd be surprised to learn how many important 'names' in the movie colony, people who have made a fine living out of the business for many years, show not the slightest interest in seeing the finished product."

San Francisco Chronicle

Stage – Screen

Young Hollywood Stars Flabbergast the Veterans

By Jimmy Fidler

HOLLYWOOD, Jan. 5, 1940 – A chat with the young stars of today leaves the veteran Hollywoodite flabbergasted. Their perspective is entirely different from their glamorous predecessors—they are aiming for goal.

Today, the average young star is fighting for true-to-life parts: characters that are a mixture of virtues and faults. For instance, consider Louis Hayward and Ida Lupino, with whom I talked with yesterday. They're typical. He was in ecstasies about an unsympathetic role in "My Son, My Son." She is praying that her hell-cat role in "The Light That Failed" will bring her more roles like it.

When I tried to argue that such parts might alienate fans they stared at me as if I might of gone mad. "But those are the parts that give an actor a real opportunity!"

The net result of this new attitude is bound to better pictures. Their relationship was more like a brother and sister than husband and wife.

"I knew Louis loved me but I was always afraid I would come home and find him with someone else. At this point, I continued to stay married to him, hoping Louis would be faithful to me. You would ask why? I liked the idea of being married but I knew our marriage was in trouble," Ida added.

WESTERN UNION
BEVERLY HILLS CALIF MAY 21 AM
MISS IDA LUPINO
SHERRY-NETHERLANDS HOTEL NYK-

A TINY PART OF YOU IN A YELLOW JACK-
ET SLIPPED GRACEFULLY UNDER MY DOOR

LAST NIGHT THANK YOU. I SAT ALONE IN YOUR HOUSE FOR TWO HOURS THIS EVENING PLAYING BACHS HEBREW RHAPSODY. UNDER THESE CIRCUMSTANCES SLIGHT NOSTALGIA INEVITABLE YOUR BRILPRESENCE HAS ALREADY PERMEATED THE PLACE STIMULATING AND WONDERFUL GIRL. KEEP YOUR HEAD AND ASPIRATIONS HIGH AND NEVER FALTER IN YOUR GOOD TASTE. LET NO NEBULOUS UNIMPORTANT EMOTION ROB YOU OF ALL THOSE THINGS STANLEY BEQUEATHED YOU. PERHAPS MY JOB IS DONE AND YOU HAVE OUTRUN ME. YET ALWAYS REMEMBER LOVE CAN FUNCTION STANDING ON THE SIDE LINES SO BABY I'LL BE WATCHING AND CHEERING YOU ON, AND IF ANY CHARACTER FORGETS MARQUIS OF QUEENSBURY RULES LET HIM BEWARE. GOD BE WITH YOU. ABOUT THIS TIME CALIFORNIA IS ENVYING NEW YORK. GO TO IT GIRL

LOUIS.

At the time of World War II, before the attack on Pearl Harbor, Louis Hayward joined the Marines. While off duty in New Zea-

land, he went under the name "Captain Richards" to avoid his lady fans, as per a waiter at The Green Parrot Restaurant.

Hayward served in the Pacific and was in charge of the photographic section. Louis directed the filming of *With the Marines at Tarawa,* a graphic documentary that earned him an Academy Award in 1945. He was also awarded a Bronze Star for his courageous service in the Marine Corps, at the United States Naval Hospital in Corona, where he was being treated for malaria.

Hayward was even awarded a Presidential Citation from FDR.

Louis Hayward's return to Hollywood was initially successful with the box office hit *And Then There Were None* (1945), an excellent version of Agatha Christie's play, *Ten Little Indians.* Louis gave a good performance as the hero opposite June Duprez.

Thursday, November 11, 1948 Omaha World-Herald
(Omaha, Nebraska)
New Films Reviewed–
FBI Smashes Secret Ring
Spies Toppled When Action Starts
By Jake Rachman

"Walk A Crooked Mile" Brandeis – The methodical, machine-like operation of the FBI is the real hero in this interesting crook picture. Here we have a partial documentary treatment of a subject that a lot of people know yet do not understand. Scenes at Los Angeles and San Francisco are taken on the spot. The plot has to do

Walk A Crooked Mile (1948) Columbia Pictures Dennis O'Keefe, Louis Hayward and Louise Allbritton

Walk A Crooked Mile **(1948) Columbia Pictures Louis Hayward and Dennis O'Keefe**

with an international spy ring that is trying to get hold of Uncle Sam's atomic secrets. These are locked up in a research laboratory which the FBI has to guard. Two special operatives, Dennis O'Keefe of the FBI and Louis Hayward of Scotland Yard, are assigned to the case after a laboratory guard has been murdered. Assisting cast is headed by Louise Allbritton, Carl Esmond, Onslow Stevens, Raymond Burr, Art Baker, Philip Van Zandt, and Lowell Gilmore.

Louis soon wandered into lackluster swashbuckling roles yet again with *The Black Arrow* (1948) co-starring with Janet Blair. The film was produced by Grant Whytock and Edward Small, and di-

The Black Arrow (1948) **Louis Hayward (Richard Shelton) and Janet Blair (Joanna Sedly).**

rected by Gordon Douglas. The story tells of an ill-starred romance between Sir Richard Shelton (Louis Hayward) and Joanna Sedley (Janet Blair). There is hatred and jealousy between the followers of the White and Red roses, which causes dual battles.

Robert Louis Stevenson's characters really live, personified as vividly as they are by these two powerful and outstanding stars, along with the powerful supporting cast. The dignified and somber castles of medieval times are intriguing backgrounds for Janet Blair, as she appears in rich elegant brocade gowns. The exotic tapestry of history forms a backdrop for Louis Hayward's portrayal of the noble knight.

The Black Arrow Louis Hayward (Richard Shelton).

The Black Arrow **Louis Hayward (Richard Shelton).**

Sunday, August 14, 1949 Charleston New and Courier Charleston,
South Carolina

THE HAMMY KNOCK

HOLLYWOOD, (AP): It happened on the "House by The River" set. On one side of the door Louis Hayward had just strangled the housemaid and was trying to stuff the body into a sack tossing it out the window into the river.

In front of the door stood Lee Bowman, unaware of the goings on inside.

"Knock six times," suggested Director Fritz Lang. "It'll make for more suspense."

The cameras turned but Bowman, nervous from long rehearsal, rapped seven times.

"Cut!" shouted Lang. Then, tongue in cheek, he said;

"Just like an actor always padding his part."

The most notorious gentleman of the road lives again; that daring highwayman of the eighteenth century came back to life recently when Louis Hayward, Columbia Pictures' star from Hollywood, visited this country to film location scenes for Dick Turpin's Ride. Here you see Louis as Dick Turpin, ready to ride to York or anywhere else his fancy takes him. Incidentally, producer Harry Joe Brown filmed most of his scenes in the grounds of Ashridge College and Ashridge Park in Hertfordshire and Midhurst in Sussex, England.

Saturday, August 30, 1952 San Diego Union
(San Diego, California)
The Aftermath of War

Capt. Louis Hayward, U.S.M.C. and Ida Lupino have a large group of friends from every age, married and single and his absence did not break up the group that drifts in and out of Ida's cottage, just as they use to do at Brentwood. Her mother, Connie, lives there and her sister, Rita, is often there as well.

Ida always has a hundred irons in the fire. She is making pictures, she is writing plays, Ida is composing music, she is arranging and rehearsing skits for camp shows, she is studying scripts, reading plays she might do, writing reams to Louis about whatever was going on last night, and demanding his opinions and advice. She gives parties usually the same day they occur to her and goes to dinners, shows or parties if she remembers she was asked in time to get there.

In their private life, Ida Lupino divorced Louis Hayward on May 11, 1945. Ida made an emotional two-minute court appearance with a charge of extreme mental cruelty, to obtain her divorce from Louis. He had been honorably discharged from the Marine Corps as a Captain.

"Louis told me he could not be tied down to one woman!"

- Ida Lupino

Personal Letter from Louis to Ida in his unique typed style:

Wednesday

Little one… You see how impossible the whole thing is… I realize this morning when you did not want me to stay in the house that it was no good… I don't blame you at all, because my behavior was rather absurd… but that is the way I get when I am with you… you have stood for a great deal of this kind of thing and it really makes me terribly sad, but there is nothing I can do about myself… You see the very last thing I want to do is hurt you in anyway at all, I continue to do so as it appears… This MUST cease… And there seems only the one course open… When you take this step, I shall see that you are protected, because it is wrong for anyone to drag you down, and make you appear as a dreadful character… I shall tell the press that it was something we decided to do long before I went overseas… Darling I REALLY am sorry that I behaved in such an abject way, but you know why I do, and there is nothing I can do about it, except to get out of your life once and for all… Believe me I will never hurt anybody the way I said last night or this morning… I am a complete nitwit to talk like that…sorry.

… Darling, darling… I ask you to forgive me, and you better pray that you NEVER meet anyone who loves you in the heart breaking, and dreadful way I do…

Louis

Hayward's mental condition was a shock to Ida when he returned home.

"I was waiting to hear from him and I thought it would be weeks or possibly months but one day the telephone rang and it was Louis. He was coming home. I

went to meet him at the airport and was followed by a
group of news men. I nervously waited for him to appear—there he was all dressed up in his Marine uniform.
I was shocked when I saw him, no longer was he that
matinee idol but an older tired looking Louis. He smiled
at me but I knew something was terribly wrong. I remember Louis was silent in the car returning home with
me. After a few days, he was still not his vibrant and loving self—he was depressed and withdrawn. Harry Mines
came to visit us, a very dear old chum of ours. He seemed
shocked by Louis' condition.

Louis replied to him, 'It is a funny thing saying good bye in my
own home.'

When Louis returned home, in January 1944, he has
been suffering from Malaria and he was hospitalized at
the naval hospital in Corona, California. I was at his bed-
side."

—*Ida Lupino*

Anyone that knew Ida and the couple's differences knew her
intimate attentions were prompted from sincere love. The temperamental differences of Ida and Louis had been generally known to
their associates in Hollywood for a number of years—both were
individualists. They got on each other's nerves, no matter how much
respect they had for each other's artistic ability.

Louis was experiencing severe psychological effects from exposure to warfare, especially shell fire. His unit had to photograph all of this and it severely affected Louis. He escaped death twice when a bullet passed through his shirt and later a piece of shrapnel pierced his helmet. Later he used it as a flower pot.

When Captain Hayward was released from the hospital the couple took the step they were contemplating three years prior but postponed by the war. Hayward moved into separate quarters. Louis was scheduled to receive an early discharge from the Marines.

"I loved him deeply but he was no longer the man I married. I was deeply crushed when he asked me to divorce him. I was unable to do the picture "The Very Thought of You". And, I went into retirement for three months."

—*Ida Lupino*

Columnist Hedda Hopper wrote about the couple in her column the week of July 21st, 1944.

"Ida has been a perfect angel to me. When we were first married, we shared the expense of our home. There is no one more considerate. I hoped we could have worked it out before I went into the service. We were having trouble then and hoped we could work it out. It is just one of those things.'"

– *Louis Hayward*

In later years, Louis' discussed openly his divorce from Ida.

"Actually the increase in divorce rate is not an abrupt statistic but one that has been advancing steadily over the last one hundred and fifty years. Furthermore, no radical change in morals is the cause for most domestic turbulence. People change and that's why divorce is sometimes the only solution. I refuse to believe that only misery results from divorce. Even though I am bitterly criticized for saying it.

Oddly enough, women, who are necessarily implicated in such an idea sometimes have very little to do with it. To be specific, in my one case, I as a person was the one who's attitudes, needs, and hopes for the future changed completely during my first marriage. If anyone would have told me, when I joined the Marine Corps, that the war would terminate my marriage of eight exhilarating years with Ida Lupino, I would have scoffed. So would she.

Yes, after I had been away for four years during which I learned too much about the brutality and the boredom of war, loneliness and fear, comradeship and homesickness, fury and anguish and useless tears. Ida agreed with me that the change in me made us strangers. Friendly strangers, to be sure but two people totally lacking those common interests which give a marriage meaning.

There are some things that can never be returned to their former state. I changed too radically, I'm much more selfish than I use to be. Before I went away I was indulgent with everyone. I shrugged things off. When I was in the service, I was blazing with anger at what damage can be done by such an attitude.

I use to be tolerant of wasted ability, of mistaken concepts, of indifference but now I am not tolerant at all. I am not even nice. I have noticed that a critical man is not in pressing social demand. In the old days, privacy did not seem important. A gang in for cocktails, half a dozen extra places at dinner and a series of guests made life exciting. As long as food and liquor and talk held up everyone was pleased. I did prefer a quieter private life!

I do not take the motion picture industry as seriously now as I did before the war. In those days, Ida was zooming into stardom at Warner Bros. Every time she came home with jubilant news about some wonderful new part she had been given, I began to talk impatiently of returning to the theatre in New York! My trouble was partly that I was a little jealous of Ida's triumph. I thought the problem over carefully since and I have concluded an aching love-envy cannot be avoided between a man and wife in the same profession, unless they are equal partners.

I was dissatisfied with the pictures in which I was cast, feeling that I was not being given enough scope. Remembering that when I was sweating out machine gun fire on a beachhead used to give me a sour laugh. There is no limit to a man's scope when he is sighting down a carbine at something moving steadily in the shadows three hundred yards away. I was unsure about my future in pictures!

Both partners should not be exhausted at the same time. I would come from the studio after having a depressing day, only to find Ida had endured an experience even more infuriating than mine. We used to make a production of our chagrin, hammering all over the house. It was fun but it was also deflating to a male ego not to get all of the sympathy."

—Louis Hayward

Ida's well known temper did not help the Hayward marriage, nor did the rumors of male suitors at their home when Louis was overseas, such as Helmut Dantine and Basil Rathbone. Ida claimed these were just two of her "chums." She had starred with Rathbone in *The Adventures of Sherlock Holmes*.

"If Louis heard I was sitting nun-like inside four walls while he was fighting he would think I'd taken leave of my senses. Louis and I have a complete understanding. There is not a jealous bone in his body. Louis knows I would not take a second look at any other man on earth. And, by the way it is very bad psychology to encourage

the idea of jealousy. It is poison in the mind. "I have always worked. I love it and I am frightfully fortunate that
I have work to do at this time."

—*Ida Lupino*

In the Marine Corps training Louis Hayward had met men
from every locality in the United States and from every profession.
Louis learned about different customs and he assimilated sectional
idioms. He became aware of the immensity of the world and had
finally grown and become his own man.

Chapter Five
The Battle of Tarawa

ON DECEMBER 6, 1941, Louis Hayward became a United States Citizen and on the following day, December 7, 1941 the Japanese attacked Pearl Harbor. This forced the United States to enter World War II and to halt the advance of the Japanese in the Pacific. Following victories at Midway Island in June 1942 and Guadalcanal in February 1943, the Gilbert Islands became the U.S. Marines' next target.

In early 1942, Louis enlisted in the United States Marine Corps.

"War is a hateful thing. The sooner it is over, the better we shall all feel," he said. "Especially today when the
horrors are not limited to certain areas, but may be thrust
upon the innocent, almost helpless civilian population."

- Louis Hayward

He completed basic training in Quantico, Virginia. He was assigned to the photographic division operating in the Pacific theatre
of war.

"With the invasion news I was frightened and worried sick
about Louis. His letters had stopped coming. The last one I received
from him was from New Zeeland. I kept current by the newspaper
accounts I had studied nursing, staying up late hours studying from
medical text books. I even joined the Women's Ambulance and De-
fense League," declared Ida Lupino.

Operation Galvanic concentrated on securing the Island of Betio in the Tarawa Atoll, situated 2,500 miles southwest of Hawaii.
The heavily fortified island was seen as an easy target by the U.S.,
but the Japanese Admiral Keiji was equally confident in his troop's
ability to maintain control and defeat the U.S. Marines. The United
States seized the fortified island of Betio from the Japanese as they
began their Central Pacific Campaign.

The Battle of Tarawa was fought over the course of three days
from November 20–23, 1943. Coral reefs snagged the U.S. landing crafts in the low tides and the Marines were forced to aban-

don their boats, wading through chest-high water as the Japanese
coastal guns pounded the shore. Among the Marines braving the
low tide that day was Captain and Photographic Officer Charles
Louis Hayward. He was in charge of fifteen officers and men of
the second Marine Division's Photographic Section fighting on the
front lines at Tarawa. Assisting Captain Hayward was Warrant Officer John Frederick Leopold. Hayward carried two 16 mm cameras loaded with Kodachrome film and was responsible for the battle footage of the resulting documentary film *With The Marines At
Tarawa*, alongside combat cameraman Sgt. Norman Hatch USMC
and numerous other Marine photographers.

Hayward spent sixteen months in the military service following
his enlistment on July 1, 1942 and spent many months training the

photographers. In an undated letter to Ida Lupino, written before he was promoted to Captain (Assistant D2, 2nd Marine Division) Hayward expressed his frustration with the mail censors.

The letter was typed by Hayward in his unique form below:

This letter may be held up, as God only knows when I'll be near a censor who can do the necessary 'looking over this effort'... In the old days I could do my own censoring but now the Powers that Be, insist on all officers below the rank of Major, having their mail looked at... Why they think that officers are more to be trusted than we 'humble folk' Jesus only knows... however that's the service for you...

Heigh Ho.

It is four days away from our anniversary, and I feel a trifle low being away from the States... I would have liked to have gone shopping for something for my 'little one' but that too is an impossibility in this region. It's a wonderful idea for you to take six months away from the grind... and it should do you a great deal of good particularly if you have learned to RELAX and consequently can add a few pounds to that fragile little frame of yours...

I wonder how you'll look when we shall see each other ... Recent studio pictures of you, don't mean anything and so I can't really tell from these. I guess you are still a pretty thing... I wonder what we'll do when this whole dreary business is over... I'm seriously thinking of leaving the States for a year or so—perhaps I'll go to South America and try and figure out "a place in the world"... I certainly want to be more of use to people, than I was in Hollywood: I'll need a year away from everything, to get a line on myself...By the way, if you happen to hear in the studios of that Gilded City... of a good 16mm sound camera for sale, you might cable me the particulars and price... A Wall Single System Sound job would do...or better still...a Berndt-Maurer camera...these might run into a few thousand dollars...but I expect...also if you hear of a good buy in the way of a boat...such as a 50ft yawl, ketch, or sloop...please let me know at once. Incidentally, you can tell the "jerk" that they wanted my unit number that there's no such thing for a Marine officer... My MAIL ADDRESS IS CORRECT, NOW, AND ALWAYS FOR ALL COMMUNICATIONS...via the heading on this letter...Tell that silly Bastard...he's crazy...

A great deal of love for you my little "poppet"

Two or three things stand out in my mind, as important things for one's morals... here they are... 'The whole earth is the sepulcher of famous men, they are commemorated not only by columns and inscriptions in their own country but in foreign lands; also by memorials graven not on stones, but on the hearts of men'

'The next time Frank Sinatra sings in the Hollywood Bowl, I hope they flush it'…..

And Love is grand

But Nature's tricky:

Watch out, girls,

Cause here comes Dickey,

Give my fondest to all the lads and lassies in that fair city…I do hope things are not too tough for 'em…

'voir Baby Mine….

My fondest love,
Louis

By the time Ida Lupino received a telegram dated April 15, 1943 from Lt. Chris Gugas USMC of the 3rd Marine Division and Fleet based in San Francisco, Louis Hayward had been promoted to Captain.

Dear Miss Lupino:

You don't know who I am but I promised your husband, Louie, that I would write you and let you how he is coming along. We came over on the same boat together and spent many pleasant days enjoying all the comforts of home… almost! Well, anyway when we got to our destination we had quite a time looking over all that we could. Louie was pretty well known here and it didn't take very long for the fact to get around that a star was in

town. He took it in his stride and spent most of the time signing in little books. Even here they go for that stuff.

Well anyway, I guess you want to know how he is doing. He was doing well until he made Captain, which he didn't want. He really was modest about the whole thing and we all admired him. I want to tell you that you want to be proud of him because he's just the kind of fellow that makes a damn good Marine. You should be very proud of him. Well, I got that off my chest, so he can't say I didn't write to you. Louie isn't here at the present, he was detached but I can say he sure does miss you and he sure wishes you were here with him.

P. S. He is swearing like a good Marine!

His letter and telegram in a pre-Pearl Harbor world could not envision the battle that lay ahead at Tarawa. It was Hayward's first taste of combat.

"It is worse than anything we had seen before. Many of us had been at Guadalcanal. Had taken pictures under fire there but you can't speak of the two in the same breath," commented Warrant Officer Leopold.

As the filming progressed, the lives of combat photographers Lieutenant Ernest A. Matthews of Dallas, Texas and Staff Sgt. Wesley Lee Kroenung, Jr. of Los Angeles were lost at the pier and valuable equipment lost in the surf - 900 still photographs and 5,000 feet of color footage showed the landing on the Atoll.

"The photographic detachment was under the direction of Capt. Charles A. Hayward. Before the landing, we photographers stayed with the leathernecks throughout the entire 76 hours of fighting.

"Our cameramen were everywhere, in the Higgins boats, on the beach, all over the island. The pictures they took show the difficulties under which they worked. Many of them had to alternate between their pistols and cameras. Our combat photographers deserve the highest commendation. Like every Marine who took part in the attack they were fighting men first," concluded Leopold.

Captain Hayward also paid tribute to his combat photographers.

"About the men at the Second Marine Division's photographic staff who fought for their lives and for the pictures made at Tarawa, little needs to be said. Their pictures tell an eloquent story of a very hazardous job. As

Marines, the men did honor to their country and their corps. As photographers, they honored their profession. No one could ask more valiant, more capable workmen than those, it was my privilege to command at Tarawa."

Captain Louis Hayward
Photographic Officer
Second Marine Division
Fleet Marine Force

The 18,000 Marines eventually overpowered the 4,500 Japanese troops after a 76-hour battle that took over 1,000 U.S. Servicemen's lives and over 4,000 Japanese. Secretary for the Navy Colonel Knox, explained the heavy American casualties at Tarawa.

The Marines had to storm ashore through treacherous coral reefs and high surf which played havoc with the light invasion craft, then found themselves on a barren exposed beach which offered no cover against the Japanese fire.

Lieutenant Cornel Carlson added, "The heaviest naval shellfire failed to wipe out the strong Japanese defenses because of their fine engineering. The walls of pillboxes were five feet thick."

Commander of the amphibious forces Major-General Holland McTyeire Smith stated, "The Japanese gun fire was so concentrated that I counted 105 dead Marines in a space of less than 20 yards."

The Marines overcame the enemy despite the initial resistance, and the Japanese garrison was destroyed. Colonel Meritt Edson said, "Everyone sees dead Japanese—ruins of burn-out block

houses, in the surf and where they had been posted as snipers." scattered among the palms.

A correspondent for the United Press praised the bravery of the Marines, "The heroism of the Marine Officers and men was almost beyond belief."

Repeatedly and unflinchingly they charged up the beach at the Japanese positions, ignoring the deadly fire. Four thousand Imperial Marines, the elite of the Japanese forces, defended Tarawa. In a four hour push, the Americans, supported by naval gun fire and dive-bombers, cleared a vital airstrip and thrust back the Japanese to a small blockhouse on the north coast, where the Japanese showed no sign of surrendering. The smell of death was everywhere.

President Roosevelt personally granted permission for the release of the film despite graphic and upsetting footage of dead

American Marines on the Battlefield. *Time-Life* photographer Robert Sherrod recommended the film to Roosevelt and was pivotal in it obtaining a nationwide release on March 2, 1944 by Universal Pictures in co-operation with the War Activities committee of the motion picture industry. The result was a surge in War Bonds.

The Battle of Tarawa Documentary

The documentary opens with the Second Marine division embarking on their transport to Tarawa. A destroyer brings sealed orders of their objective as the Marines are attended by Father Kelly.

Warships bombard the island with gunfire as Navy planes bomb and strafe. 4,000 lbs. of explosives were dropped on the island prior to landing.

The Marines are hit by heavy machine gun fire and mortar fire from the enemy before wading ashore from wrecked amphibians. A long pier offers some protection but Japanese fire pins the Marines down for hours. Blood plasma saves lives before reinforcements arrive and they move forward inland. The Japanese are out of sight, hidden behind trees, buried in pillboxes and bunkers.

Hand grenades, flame throwers, gunfire and mortars are used to flush out the enemy. A Japanese bunker is blown up and the carnage shown in gory detail.

The Narrator announces, "They are savage fighters. Their lives mean nothing to them."

The Japanese swarm out at night swimming to the wrecked amphibians in order to set up machine guns.

The documentary shows the brutality of war with dead Marines scattered along the beach and floating in the sea. It doesn't glorify the battle but it does show the bravery of the Marines.

"This is the price we have to pay for the war we didn't want," declares the narrator.

Meanwhile, *With The Marines at Tarawa* received excellent reviews. Jack O'Brien of the Associated Press wrote, "Technically the picture is a fine job… Even the most horrible scenes deleted, it is far and away the most powerful war document this reviewer has ever seen to date… the sight of The American boys, wounded and dead, are enough to make an honest pacifists a bloody thirsty Revenger."

The Academy Award

In March 1945 the annual Academy of Motion Arts and Sciences ceremony at Grauman's Chinese Theatre awarded *With The Marines At Tarawa* an Academy Award for Best Documentary Short. The award went to The Marine Corps for their collective effort rather than uncredited director Captain Louis Hayward.

"Tireless leadership, painstaking efforts and devotion to duty," stated the award of the Bronze Star Medal for Marine Captain Charles Louis Hayward, who is responsible for the excellent photographic record of the Marine assault on Tarawa.

The Oscar that was presented to the Marine Corps and a replica Oscar is displayed at the National Museum of the Marine Corps, in Quantico, Virginia. Due to the shortage of metal during the war effort, the Academy presented the Marine Corps with a plaster statue in the shape of a tablet. It is housed at the same museum but not on display. Louis Hayward did not attend the awards ceremony.

Awarded Bronze Star Medal

Chapter Six
Return to Hollywood

His RETURN TO ACTING was the excellent version of Agatha Christie's play *And Then There Were None,* his first film since his return from the war. Louis was very good as the hero opposite June Duprez, but was only one member of a powerhouse cast. Walter Huston, Barry Fitzgerald, and Judith Anderson also starred.

Hayward was then cast as a war pilot hero opposite Jane Russell, in Hunt Stromberg's *Young Widow.* This was not a good film and suffered the interference of Howard Hughes on the production end, to whom Russell was under contract. Louis and Jane Russell got along well and became lifelong friends.

The Pirates of Capri **Actress Plays Queen Binnie Barnes, London - born Hol-
lywood actress plays the part of Queen Carolina of Naples, filmed in Italy.
This film is being produced in both Italian and English. Miss Barnes and
Louis Hayward pictured with her play in both versions.**

Saturday, August 30, 1952 San Diego, California
Louis Hayward Scores In 'Captain Pirate' Film

Louis Hayward, an accomplish actor who long ago adopted the safest possible film formula, trots it over again in "Captain Pirate," which opened yesterday at the Tower Theatre. Once more he dresses up in fancy costumes, fights impressive duels with villains, overcomes long odds and end ups in the arms of a fancy woman.

The woman is Patricia Medina, a beautiful girl.

Captain Pirate is really a pseudonym for Captain Blood, that honorable brigand who has a knack for getting himself into compromising spots. This time his trouble arises when another pirate, an evil one, uses his name during a raid on a Caribbean port. Though Captain Blood's innocence seems fairly evident, he's arrested for the crime and seems destined to hang for it until Patricia leads a party of his former followers to his rescue.

The charge of piracy is ultimately proved false and the seafaring gentleman is left with a final scene promising him romance and a life of peace.

Hayward handles his agile role in live and convincing fashion but is handicapped at times by pompous, dull dialogue. Miss Medina has little to do but look beautiful, which she does. John Hutton plays the villain to the hilt.

For an adventure film "Captain Pirate" is above average. While the costume, swashbuckling dramas have

The Pirates of Capri Louis Hayward

been overdone a bit lately, there is something about pirate stories that always seems to have wide general appeal.

"I formed my own film company, being one of the first of the actors to do so. I received a percentage of the Pirate's profits for my subsequent films."

—*Louis Hayward*

"I was in Italy to co-produce and star in the swash-buckler, *Pirates of Capri*. A Scarlet type story. This was an advantage to me, although the dialogue and performance of the supporting cast left something to be desired. However, I finally realized the public preferred to see me in action adventure stories. "I had a fast succession of films, "The Fortunes of Captain Blood", "The Lady and the Bandit" and "Captain Pirate". All these films were financial successes and I co-starred with the beautiful Patricia Medina. We made a most attractive team."

—*Louis Hayward*

The Royal African Rifles followed. Louis Hayward was the Executive Producer and the star.

Ten years after completion of these films Hayward gave up one career because of his opinion that he had "outgrown" it, and started another.

"I found I'd become typed as a romantic young ad-
venturer with a sword and I felt I'd reached the awkward
age for that sort of thing, so I walked out."

—*Louis Hayward*

Louis and Peggy

Louis and Peggy Morrow Field

It was during his period of finding himself that Louis Hayward
also found Peggy Morrow, of New York City. She was living in a
Hollywood apartment and did not like it here. Peggy, encouraged

Peggy, Louis and Ida

by friends, went back to New York. Louis was looking for a place
to live after his divorce from Ida. He had been moving from hotel to hotel due to the housing shortage. Louis met Peggy and it
was a happy beginning, and the evening proved to be a rewarding
one, filled with good conversation and laughter. As Louis was leaving, he suggested he and Peggy have dinner together the following
night and the two continued having dinner together every evening
for two weeks to perfect a perfect lease.

At the end of this period Peggy decided to remain in Hollywood because she had begun to find the town stimulating.

Louis was able to secure an apartment in the same building on the floor beneath Peggy. When Louis moved in he was warned that no social activities were allowed in the building. One evening Louis entertained a group of Marine Corps buddies and the very next day he was notified that eviction papers were being drawn. In keeping with his new rule of taking the long range view of everything, he decided to go to England to visit his mother.

Peggy Morrow decided to purchase a house in Beverly Hills. While Louis was away he telephoned her three times a week just to be certain she did not lose interest in him. Shortly after his return, they married quietly in 1946.

"I could not stand this woman!"

—*Ida Lupino*

Chapter Seven

The Lone Wolf
and British Television

HAYWARD, WHILE STAYING WITH MOVIES, ventured into television, not only with some ten *American Playhouse* theatre productions and episodic television through the 1960's, but with production investments of his own as well.

In 1954, Hayward produced and starred in the 39 week television series *The Lone Wolf (Streets of Danger)* after buying exclusive rights to several of Louis Joseph Vance's original *Lone Wolf* stories.

Tuesday, October 6, 1953 San Louis Obispo Daily
Telegram (San Louis Obispo, California)
HOLLYWOOD TODAY!
Movies - TV - Radio
By Erskine Johnson

HOLLYWOOD – (NES) – Behind theatre and TV screens: Hollywood first and most famous private eye, The Lone Wolf is on TV—bound in the most lavish most costly series of home screen movies ever made.

Louis Hayward will star in 78 half hour Lone Wolf films, costing $35,000 each, in a Television Programs, Inc., one of the largest telepix distributors in the country. $2,800.00 partnership deal. Jack Cross and Phil Krasne will produce the films for United.

Hayward received a percentage of the profits for the series.

In 1961, Louis began producing a television series *The Pursuers*, filmed in England. He starred in 39 episodes. Hayward has a similar deal for the British series. However, the series was not shown in the United States.

> "It was a hit over there but we foolishly made it in black and white. When we were ready for America, color was all the rage and nobody would look at it!"
>
> *– Louis Hayward*

A distinguished looking gentleman now, Louis returned grey in the wings, but not as a romantic lead with another sword buckled on a cavalry sabre. This time he appeared in the larruping Technicolor Western, *Chuka*, produced by Rod Taylor and Jack Jason in association with Paramount Pictures.

Hayward co-starred with Taylor, Ernest Borgnine, John Mills, Luciana Paluzzi, James Whitmore, and Angela Dorian under the direction of the same Gordon Douglas for whom Louis starred in *The Black Arrow*. Louis portrayed Major Benson, a charming rake and card, knifed and slain by his Indian mistress on the brink of the act of love.

Then came *The Strange Woman* with Hedy Lamarr, in which Hayward portrays a weakling. In *Repeat Performance*, he appears opposite Joan Leslie as an alcoholic. Louis appeared in the documentary-styled *Walk A Crooked Mile* as a Scotland Yard man working with FBI man Dennis O'Keefe to round up cold war spies.

The Strange Woman (1946, United Artists) Produced by Jack Chertok.
Co-starring Louis Hayward and Heddy Lamar.

"I was dissatisfied with the insularity of Hollywood and the tendency out there to confine oneself to a single social group and to resist all outside influences. I found myself wanting to talk to people who had interests outside of the motion picture industry, who could help me look at my own profession in perspective to other occupations.

I honestly believe that for some people happiness and contentment are attained only in and most fully through a second marriage. Now, I like my home to myself and my wife, Peggy. I like quiet evenings during which we chat, read and listen to music.

When I became a free man, I decided not to marry a professional woman. My ambition was to have my defeats, disappointments and disillusionments taken very seriously.

One of my mistakes in my first marriage was to go flying off alone to New York or San Francisco. I was always restless. I now know there is no real repose for me without Peggy when we are not together. It seems to me that a genuine inclination to share all things, to be a real team is the most important plan of marriage and one that some men learn only on a second try."

—Louis Hayward

The Son of Dr. Jekyll

The Son of Dr. Jekyll

There was a time in Hollywood when Louis Hayward had a reputation for being temperamental but with his second marriage he was sweet and reasonable. If he found a line of dialogue inappropriate, he discussed it calmly with the director or the writer or both and a satisfactory compromise was reached. The publicity department all adored him and freelance photographers around town really knew he was genuine, as were his friends. He became more selfish and more critical of all things in his professional life but more resigned to the vagaries of his personal life. Louis is far more responsible in both his personal and his professional attitudes. He was the head of the house, entirely responsible for the welfare of his wife and home.

Louis' marriage to Peggy lasted only four years. They were divorced in 1950. Hayward was required to pay her 12 and a half percent of his income for one year and 10 percent for the following two years.

According to Peggy's diaries, "He was very sexual and was always leaving me for someone else." She accused him of desertion.

Louis replied, "She was very needy." And he added, "That is why I believe that for a person like me divorce was the only solution."

It was rumored that they both drank way too much.

Ida Lupino asked Louis to appear in her company Filmaker's film production *The Bigamist*. Louis refused but they did remain friends throughout the years.

Louis and June

"I harbor no bad feelings toward Louis."

—*Ida Lupino*

June Hanson

June Hanson was a pure Nordic beauty, golden hair, flawless skin and a lovely figure. She had a calm relaxed manner, soothing to an artist husband, and yet she was downright honest. June was back stage with him in his dressing room and traveled with him when she could. June and Louis were both animal lovers and enjoying cooking together.

"She's wonderful. She's incredible."

　　　　　　　　　　—Louis Hayward

His marriage to June Hanson, on November 23, 1951, finally brought him a sense of stability in his private life, along with a step-son, Dana. Papers were drawn for Louis to adopt the boy but he never did sign them. Hayward never had any children of his own.

All in all, it is as perfect marriage as he could find.

"He is my career. He comes first."

　　　　　　　　　　—June Hayward

"Until I met her, I was completely incomplete."

　　　　　　　　　　—Louis Hayward

Thursday, August 9, 1956 Paper: Trenton Evening Times
(Trenton, New Jersey)
Role Of Experience

HOLLYWOOD (UP) – Actor Louis Hayward claimed he was no stranger to hypnosis when he accept-ed the male lead in "The Search For Bridey Murphy," a film about hypnosis. Flying here from New York in 1947,

In Search of Bridey Murphy

Hayward told a fellow passenger, Los Angeles business man Sol Andrews, that he had a terrible headache. Andrews, an amateur hypnotist, put Hayward to sleep for the rest of the flight and the actor arrived home feeling fine.

Date: Sunday, August 20, 1961 Springfield Union
(Springfield, Massachusetts)
At Stockbridge
Corpses Litter Stage Of Berkshire Theatre

The acknowledged master of sustained thrill and grisly surprises Agatha Christie, author of "Ten Little Indians," the corpse–strewn thriller opening Monday night at the Berkshire Playhouse in Stockbridge.

Killing Field Day

When it played for 28 months on Broadway a few years ago, this mystery–melodrama was called a "homicidal field day" right up to final curtain, with plenty of guessing about "whodunit." It was termed "the most expert of coldblooded thrillers," and rejoiced in a "fresh corpse every 10 minutes." The house of horrors with Walter Hudson, Louis Hayward, Barry Fitzgerald and Judith Anderson. The play will be seen at the Berkshire Playhouse evenings through Saturday 8:45, with matinees at Wednesday and Friday 2:30.

With Ralph Bellamy in "The Picture of Dorian Gray," a 1961 episode of the TV series *Golden Showcase*.

With George C. Scott in the TV production of "The Picture of Dorian Gray."

Monday, July 2, 1962 Omaha World Herald
Stage, Screen and TV–
Louis Hayward Reappears After Prolonged Absence

One of the viewer's favorite swashbucklers—and one of many fine talents either wasted or buffeted about Hollywood is actor Louis Hayward. He is scheduled to appear, however, next Wednesday evening on TV's "Mystery Theater."

"Mystery Theatre," of course, is what is termed by network as selected reruns of odd shows. In this program he portrays a mystery writer who joins his secretary in an attempt to murder his wife. It's not one of the greatest parts.

For the last few years, Mr. Hayward has been living in England, apparently tired of obtaining such eminent screen projects as "The Search for Bridey Murphy," an exploitation dish of trash that was released in 1956. It was his last film.

In 1963, Hayward returned to the stage again, this time joining the touring company of the musical *Camelot*, and cut a swath across the country portraying King Arthur, the Richard Burton role. He co-starred with Kathryn Grayson and Arthur Treacher. This road show production was well received.

Louis appeared in Paramount Picture's outdoors adventure drama *Chuka* (1967) which stars Rod Taylor, Luciana Paluzzi, John

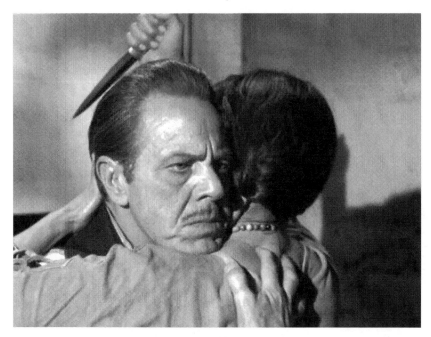

Chuka

Mills, Ernest Borgnine, James Whitmore and Joseph Sirola. Chuka is the story behind the last stand of a U.S. Calvary troop in a prairie fort besieged by Indians. It was directed by Gordon Douglas.

On November 4, 1967, Louis' brother John passed away in Los Angeles, California.

Louis continued to appear in *Camelot* but was eventually forced to withdraw from the play in 1984 due to illness. He was hospitalized and underwent successful surgery. (Actor George Wallace had rushed to Chicago to replace the ailing Louis Hayward in 1964 for a prior production of *Camelot*.)

Louis only appeared occasionally on television and in films, in the later sixties and early seventies. Hayward sold his restaurant located at 8572 Sunset Blvd. He and his wife, June, purchased and made a home at 235 El Portal in Palm Springs. They also owned a

Camelot

home in Malibu 21756 Pacific Coast Hwy, which was later sold to Adam West. Hayward's hobby was painting in water colors. Louis enjoyed playing tennis and golf. Louis and June had a love for music and attended the opera and symphony concerts. They would often be seen at the theatre in Los Angeles.

Hayward bowed out of acting in the mid 1970's.

His last acting performance was in the 1973 horror film *Terror in the Wax Museum*, in which he portrayed the owner of a London pub located next door to the museum. The film co-starred contemporaries from Hayward's yester-years in Hollywood. These co-stars were Ray Milland, Elsa Lanchester, Broderick Crawford, Patric Knowles and John Carradine.

Louis was not the legend of bygone hopes but certainly a wiser and comfortable man.

> "If you are lucky, you can always make money but never make up for the time you have lost."
>
> —*Louis Hayward*

In 1983, Louis was diagnosed with lung Cancer. Hayward was a very heavy cigarette smoker his entire adult life and admitted to a three pack a day habit. His final months were spent lecturing the public on the dangers of smoking.

Louis Hayward died of lung Cancer and renal failure on February 21, 1985 at 5:50 p.m., at the Desert Hospital in Palm Springs, California. He was 75 years old. Hayward was cremated by The

Neptune Society the very next day. June Hayward scattered his ashes at a non-disclosed location.

> "My last wish is for the public to know what terrible pain comes from Cancer and then they would never smoke another cigarette."
>
> *—Louis Hayward*

At Hayward's request, there was no funeral or memorial service. Louis had even destroyed artifacts of his career. It was reported, he burned them in his backyard, thinking they were not important or of any value.

Actor Joseph Sirola spoke highly of Hayward, "He was a wonderful man. I met him and his wife, June, in Rome. They were staying at the The Residence Palace. Louie told me when I came to Los Angeles to give him a call. I did and he asked me where I was staying. I told him I had not decided. His response, 'You are staying with us at Malibu.' I was there for six months. June was an Angel. She did everything for him. My favorite film of his was 'Man in the Iron Mask.' He was a very good actor. We worked together in the film 'Chuka.' The perfect gentleman!"

On the set

Afterword
by Barry Lane

THE TITLE OF THIS, *Beyond The Iron Mask,* could not have been anything else.

Louis Hayward could have been, within the content of the entertainment industry, not only something else, but several other somethings.

After the Academy Award for *With The Marines At Tarawa,* Best Short Documentary, as Director, the door was open for Louis at both Warner's and Fox. Later, only slightly less so at CBS, during the heyday of movies made for television.

I have no single memory, for me it is all of a piece. This guy was not only good company, the best, kind, generous and funny as hell. Just a pleasure to know. I absolutely loved him and by extension the entire family.

By intuition and inclination, I had for a long, long time been preparing myself for a place in the business, playing either a suave detective or pirate captain. Meanwhile, I needed a job and after some work in television news and theatrical public relations, I landed at GAC – General Artists Corporation. At the time *Camelot* was up. As it happened, they represented Katheryn Grayson, Louis Hayward and Arthur Treacher.

I believe the entirety of the Lerner & Lowe organization. I was the low man on the totem pole but we did get to a performance. I took a young woman from my office with me. One moment in his dressing room, while Louis was mixing a scotch highball with his index finger, she asked, "Why are you not in pictures any longer?" He answered honestly, that he wasn't being asked. After an appropriate and uncomfortable pause, we left. I went back a week or ten days later and had a somewhat more productive meeting with him.

By the time, I came along in Louis Hayward's career as a film star, it had reached its inevitable conclusion. It can be charted or bookended by his appearance as *The Saint In New York,* a light hearted, stylish, and original second feature that gave birth to the Series. Fifteen years later, a second, dry and workmanlike appearance.

In between came all the films, we loved in the five years prior to the war, and five years following it. *Duke of West Point, Man In The*

Iron Mask, Son of Monte Cristo, And Then There Were None. A kind of reprise on his I*ron Mask* performance in *The Pirates of Capri. Son of Dr. Jekyll* was his masterpiece.

Changing times lead to television, something Louis always considered a mistake. *The Lone Wolf,* in the United States was followed by *The Pursuers,* in Britain. Between these came an offer to play in *Robin Hood* which was declined. A pair of pilots, *The Highwayman* and *The Louis Hayward Show,* in which he played an aging movie star opposite Lita Milan.

And, then I came along. *The Survivors* happened and probably could have been a personal success if it had been a success at all.

As a child, I do mean at age ten or so and then as a young man, I related to Louis Hayward. I was a young man with stars in his eyes, too. I loved him and nothing ever happened to damage or alter that feeling. Rather the opposite, I feel the same way as this is being written, we had a lot of fun. I still find it hard to explain the special quality that set him aside from anyone else.

The Films of Louis Hayward

Self Made Lady (1932) Paul Geneste

The Man Outside (1933) Frank Elford

I'll Stick To You (1933) Ronnie Mathews

Sorrell and Son (1933) Duncan

The Thirteenth Candle (1933) Paul Marriott

Chelsea Life (1933) David Fenner

The Love Test (1935) John Gregg

The Flame Within (1935) Jack Kerry

A Feather In Her Hat (1935) Richard Orland

Trouble for Two (1936) The young man with the cream tarts

Anthony Adverse (1936) Denis Moore

The Luckiest Girl In The World (1936) Anthony McClellan

The Woman I Love (1937) Lt. Jean Herbillion

Condemned Woman (1938) Dr. Phillip Duncan

The Saint In New York (1938) Simon Templar

The Rage of Paris (1938) Bill Duncan

The Duke of West Point (1938) Steve Earley

Midnight Intruder (1938) Barry Gilbert posing as John Clark Reitter, Jr.

The Man In The Iron Mask (1939) Louis XIV/ Philippe of Gascony

Dance, Girl, Dance (1940) Jimmy Harris

The Son of Monte Cristo (1940) Edmond Dantes, Jr.

My Son, My Son! (1940) Oliver Essex

Ladies In Retirement (1941) Albert Feather

And Then There Were None (1945) Phillip Lombard

Young Widow (1946) Lt. Jim Cameron

The Strange Woman (1946) Ephraim Poster

The Return of Monte Cristo (1946) Edmond Dantes

Repeat Performance (1947) Barney Page

Ruthless (1948) Vic Lambdin

The Black Arrow (1948) Sir Richard Shelton

Walk A Crooked Mile (1948) Phillip 'Scotty' Grayson

The Pirates of Capri (1949) Count Amalfi alias Captain Sirocco

House By The River (1950) Stephen Byrne

Fortunes of Captain Blood (1950) Captain Peter Blood

The Son of Dr. Jekyll (1951) Edward Jekyll / Dr. Henry Jekyll / Mr. Hyde

The Lady And The Bandit (1951) Dick Turpin

Captain Pirate (1952) Captain Peter Blood

The Lady In The Iron Mask (1952) D'Artagnan

The Saint's Girl Friday (1953) Simon Templar

The Royal African Rifles (1953) Denham

Duffy of San Quentin (1954) Edward 'Romeo' Harper

The Search for Bridey Murphy (1965) Morey Bernstein

The Christmas Kid (1967) Mike Culligan

Chuka (1967) Major Benson

Terror in the Wax Museum (1973) Tim Fowley

The Christmas Kid, co-starring Jeffrey Hunter.

Television Appearances

Schlitz Playhouse TV Series (1951)

    A Contest of Ladies Stephen Morley

The Ford Television Theatre (1952)

    Crossed and Double Cross Jack Redmond

The Lone Wolf (1954 – 1955)

    Series, 30 Episodes, Michael Lanyard

Climax! (1955)

    A Promise to Murder Randy Townsend

Lux Video Theatre (1955)

    Suspicion So Evil My Love Mark

TV Reader's Digest (1955)

    The Voyage of Captain Tom Jones, Pirate Captain Tom Jones

Matinee Theatre (1955)

    Beginning Now

Studio One in Hollywood (1958)

    Balance of Terror Mike Fenby

The Highwayman TV Movie (1958) James MacDonald

Riverboat (1959)

    Payment in Full Ashley Cowen

Kraft Mystery Theatre (1960 - 62)

    Dead On Nine Robert Leigh

Golden Show Case (1961)

    The Picture of Dorian Grey Basil Hallward

The Pursuers (1961 - 1962)

    Series, 40 Episodes, Detective Inspector John Bollinger

Kraft Mystery Theatre (1962)

    Dead on Nine Robert Lee

The Alfred Hitchcock Hour (1962)

    Day of Reckoning Judge David Wilcox

Rawhide (1964)

    The Backshooter John Tasker

Burke's Law (1965)

    Who Killed the Jackpot? Stacy Blackwell

The Survivors (1969)

    Series, 4 Episodes, Jonathan Carlyle

The Phynx (1970) *Louis Hayward*

Night Gallery (1970)

    Certain Shadows on the Wall Dr. Stephen Brigham

The Last of the Powerseekers (1971) TV Movie, Jonathon Carlyle

The Magician (1974)

    The Illusion of the Lethal Plaything Millots

Made in the USA
Middletown, DE
05 August 2023

36217920R00086